Print the alphabet with **uppercase** and **lowercase** letters.

Aa

Zz

Curriculum Area: Language Arts   **Skills:** Recognizing Letters, Writing

Look at the words on the apples. Print the words in **alphabetical order** on the lines.

Curriculum Area: Language Arts   **Skills:** Alphabetizing, Writing

Look at the pictures. Print the letter you hear at the **beginning** of each word.

1.	2.	3.
an	ate	oon
4.	5.	6.
ug	eal	oat
7.	8.	9.
agon	eaf	eer

Curriculum Area: Language Arts **Skills:** Recognizing Objects, Identifying Beginning Consonants

In each box, print the letter you hear at the **beginning** of each word.

1.	2.	3.
oat	ap	eat
4.	5.	6.
at	ook	ug
7.	8.	9.
un	op	ake

Curriculum Area: Language Arts **Skills:** Identifying Objects, Rhyming

Look at the pictures. Print the letter you hear at the **end** of each word.

1.	2.	3.
bu	soa	ca
4.	5.	6.
lea	lio	we
7.	8.	9.
le	dru	boo

Curriculum Area: Language Arts   **Skills:** Recognizing Objects, Identifying Final Consonants

Look at the pictures and words below. Print the missing short vowel: **a, e, i, o,** or **u.**

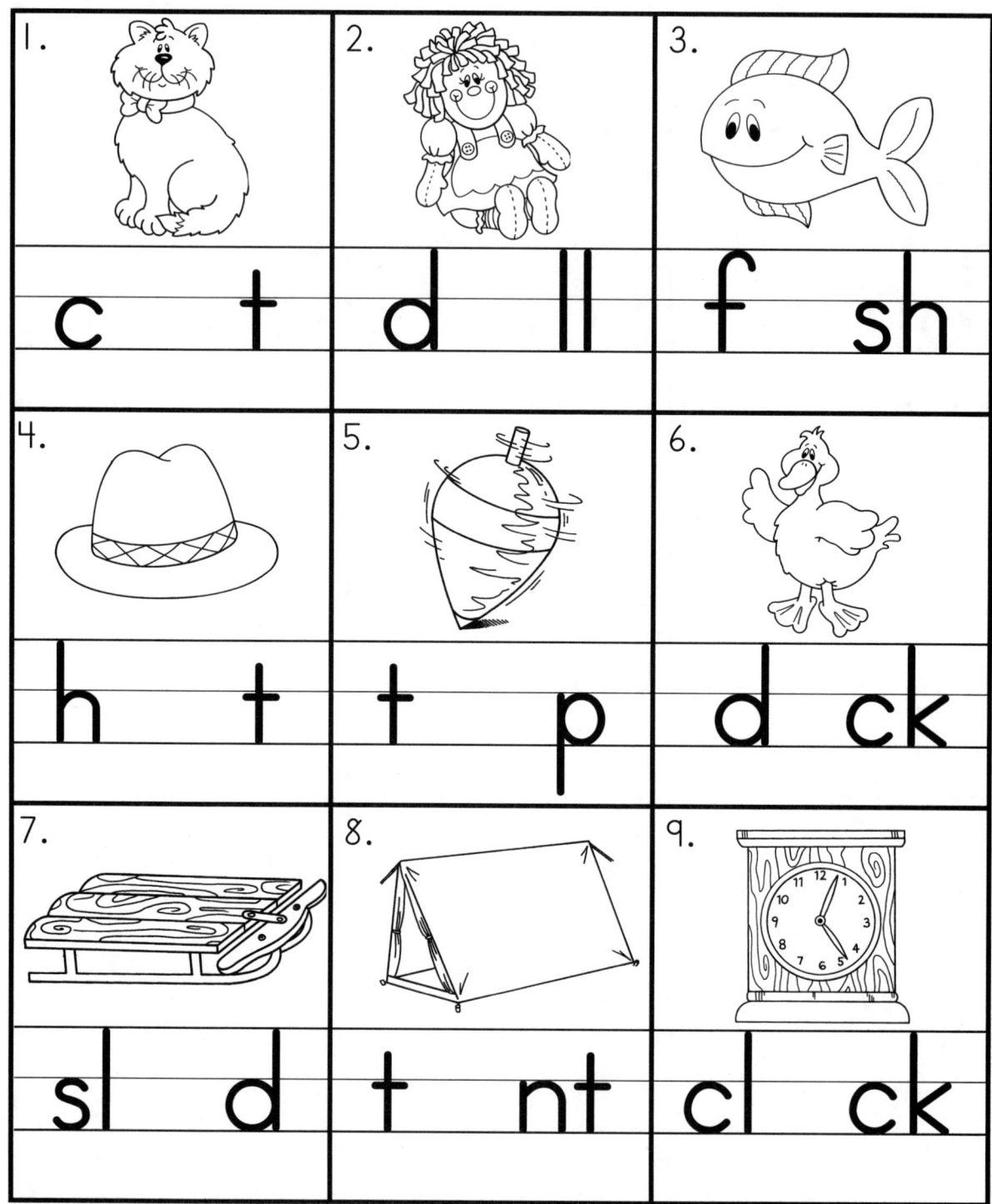

Curriculum Area: Language Arts   **Skills:** Identifying Short Vowel Sounds, Writing

A **synonym** is a word that has almost the **same** meaning as another word.
Examples: happy — glad   yell — shout

Read the words below. Find the words that are synonyms on the balloons. Color each balloon the correct color.

kind – pink
woman – purple
above – green
push – red

pal – yellow
sick – orange
large – blue
small – brown

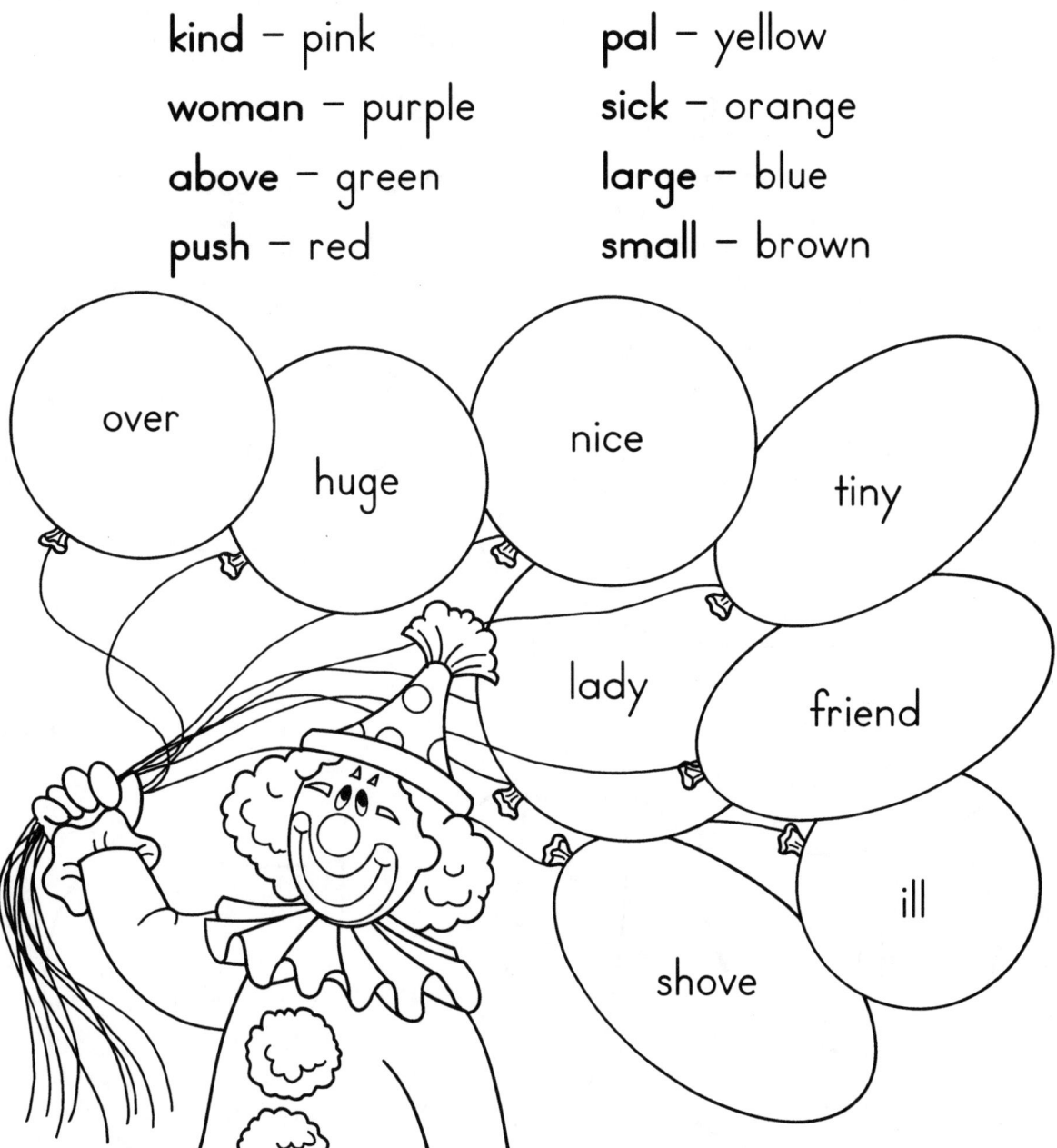

Curriculum Area: Language Arts   **Skills:** Recognizing Synonyms, Matching, Coloring

An **antonym** is a word that has the **opposite** meaning of another word.
Examples: up — down   left — right

Read the words below. Find their **antonyms** on the butterfly. Color each section the correct color.

boy – blue
little – yellow
above – green
inside – orange

go – red
last – purple
mean – brown
hard – pink

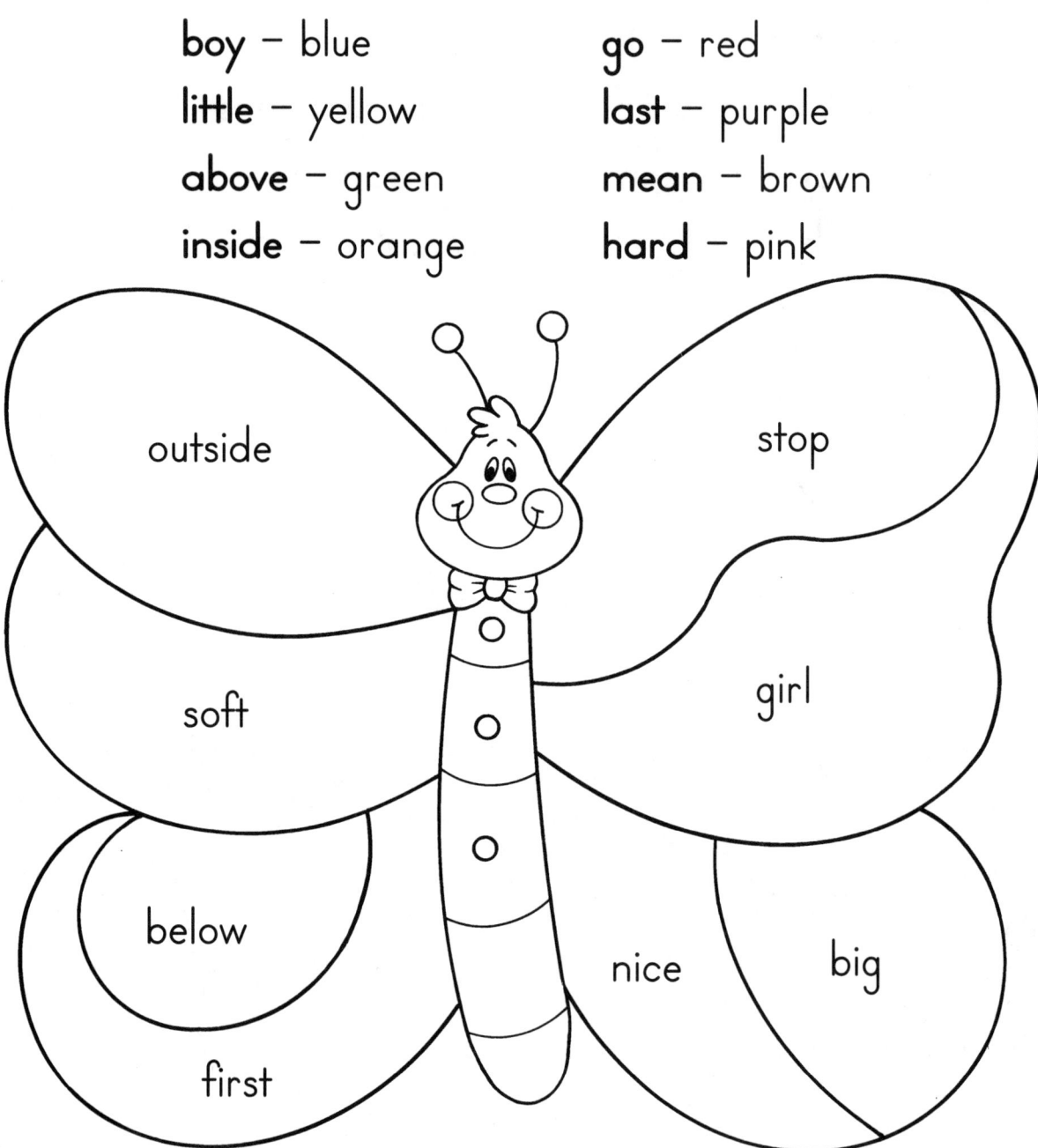

Curriculum Area: Language Arts   **Skills:** Recognizing Antonyms, Matching, Coloring

Number the following sentences in the correct order by placing a numeral in each box.

A.
- ☐ I got out of bed.
- ☐ I brushed my teeth.
- ☐ I woke up.

B.
- ☐ I fell off my bike.
- ☐ Mom gave me a bandage.
- ☐ I cut my knee.

C.
- ☐ He ran to first base.
- ☐ The pitcher threw the ball.
- ☐ The batter hit the ball.

D.
- ☐ Mom hung it on the refrigerator.
- ☐ She drew a picture.
- ☐ Susan got paper and crayons.

Curriculum Area: Language Arts   **Skills:** Sequencing

Read each sentence below. If the sentence tells about something that **could** really happen, circle the picture. If it **could not** really happen, place an X on the picture.

1. Steve played basketball.
2. Rabbit and Turtle raced.
3. The bear had a party.
4. Sue can ride a bike.
5. Snail and Worm went to school.
6. Fish can live in the ocean.

Curriculum Area: Language Arts **Skills:** Distinguishing Between Fact and Fantasy

Follow the directions below to create a drawing inside the box.

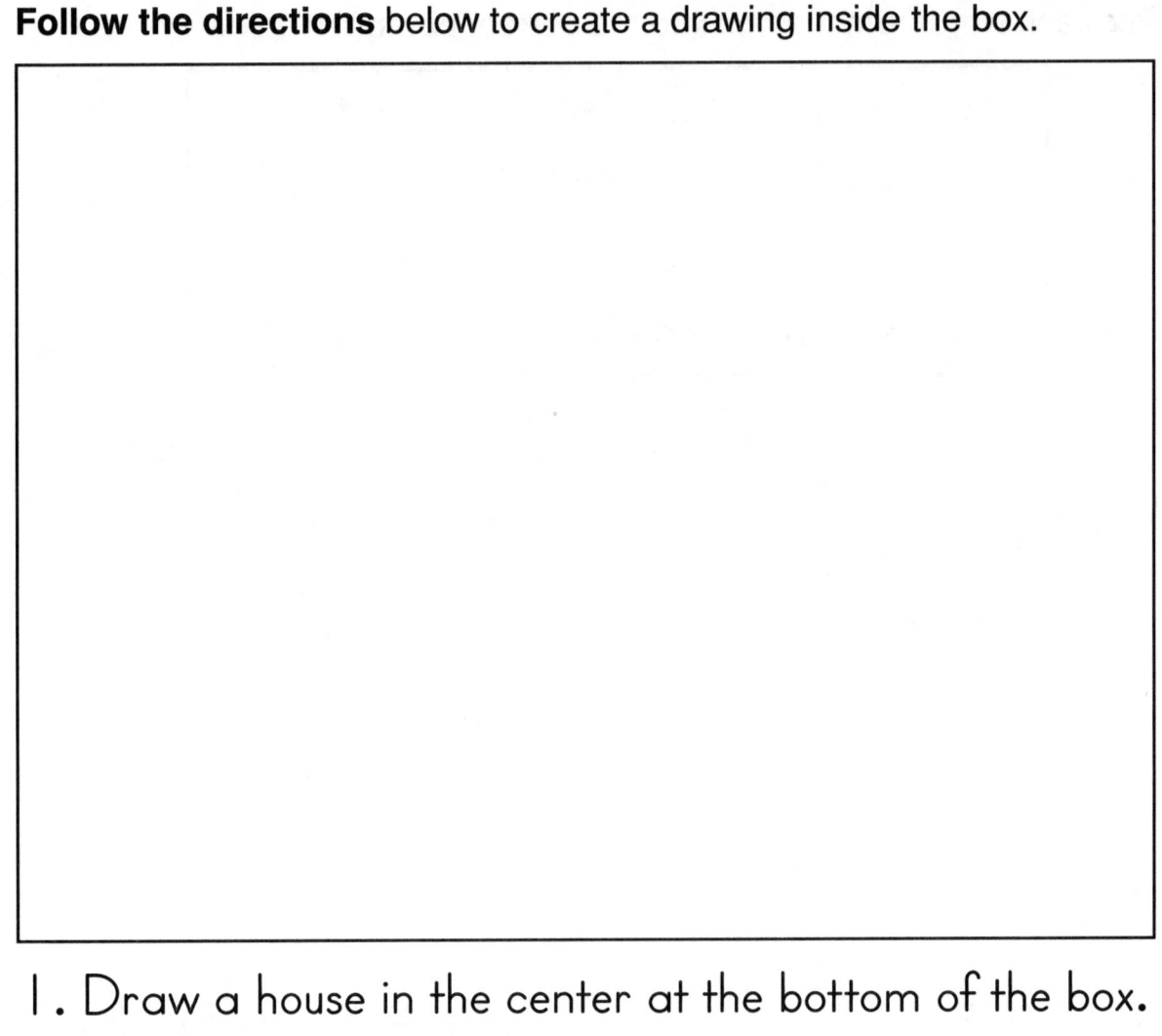

1. Draw a house in the center at the bottom of the box.
2. Draw a door and 4 windows on the house.
3. Draw two trees on the right.
4. Draw some grass.
5. Draw four flowers on the left.
6. Draw a sun.
7. Draw some clouds.

Curriculum Area: Language Arts **Skills:** Following Directions

Put each word from the box into the correct **category** below.

sunburn	Easter	sled
mittens	beach ball	pumpkins
showers	turkey	flowers
snowman	football	pool

Winter Things

1. _____

2. _____

3. _____

Spring Things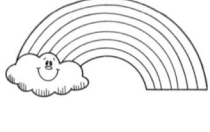

1. _____

2. _____

3. _____

Summer Things

1. _____

2. _____

3. _____

Fall Things

1. _____

2. _____

3. _____

Curriculum Area: Language Arts   **Skills:** Categorizing

Separate each compound word to make two words.

1. doghouse _____ + _____

2. football _____ + _____

3. fishbowl _____ + _____

4. sandbox _____ + _____

5. rainbow _____ + _____

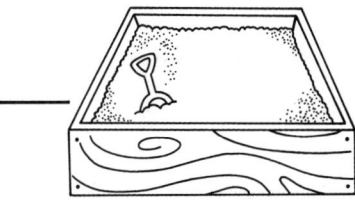

6. suitcase _____ + _____

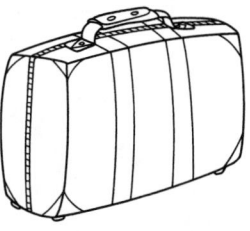

Curriculum Area: Language Arts   **Skills:** Understanding Compound Words, Writing

Circle the missing **contraction** in each sentence.

1. _____ going to read a book.

   I'm   I've

2. _____ missed the bus.

   Can't   We've

3. The baby bird _____ fly.

   isn't   couldn't

4. _____ going outside to play.

   We're   I've

5. On Saturday, _____ go to the zoo.

   we're   we'll

Curriculum Area: Language Arts   **Skills:** Distinguishing Between Contractions

Read each story. Decide what will happen **next**. Fill in the circle next to the best answer.

1. The mother bird found a good place to build a nest. She found some string. She got some grass, too. Then she used the string and grass to build the nest. After she built the nest ...

    ○ she visited friends.
    ○ she laid some eggs.
    ○ she flew away.

2. It was a sunny day. My mother made some sandwiches. My father got some chips. My brother, Bill, got some juice. I got the cookies. We put everything in a basket. Then we ...

    ○ went swimming.
    ○ went to bed.
    ○ went on a picnic.

Print the **months of the year** in order. Trace the first two which are done for you.

January   J

February   A

M   S

A   O

M   N

J   D

Curriculum Area: Language Arts   **Skills:** Identifying Months of the Year, Writing

Fill in the **days of the week** in order. Trace the first day which is done for you.

Sunday

Curriculum Area: Language Arts   **Skills:** Identifying Days of the Week, Writing

A **pronoun** is a word that can take the place of a noun or proper noun.
Example: **Susan** has a book. **She** likes to read **it**.

Use the **pronouns** in the box to fill in the blanks.

| We | He | They | She |

1. **Billy** has some skates.
   _____ likes to skate down hills.

2. **Jessica and Emily** went to the park.
   _____ like to go down the slide.

3. **Sally** has a radio.
   _____ likes to listen to music.

4. **Fred and I** found some worms.
   _____ are going fishing.

Curriculum Area: Language Arts   **Skills:** Using Plural and Singular Pronouns

Read each story. Fill in the circle next to the word that explains how each person or group **felt**.

1. The children went to the pumpkin patch. They rode in a wagon to the patch. Then they picked a pumpkin to take home. The children felt. . .
   - ○ angry
   - ○ sad
   - ○ excited

2. Tom went out to play. He took his bat, ball, and mitt. He couldn't find anyone to play with him. Tom felt . . .
   - ○ happy
   - ○ scared
   - ○ sad

3. Sally had a birthday party. She put on her new dress. She got many gifts. Sally felt . . .
   - ○ happy
   - ○ angry
   - ○ sad

Curriculum Area: Language Arts **Skills:** Reading Comprehension, Identifying Emotions

Sentences and proper nouns begin with **capital letters**.
Example: **H**ave you seen **S**teve's new bike?

Circle the words that need **capital letters**. Write the sentences correctly.

1. did judy name her kitten fluffy?

2. today is tuesday.

3. will it snow in january?

Curriculum Area: Language Arts   **Skills:** Capitalizing, Writing Sentences

Write the correct **punctuation mark** at the end of each sentence. Put a **?** or **.** in each box.

1. Have you been to the circus ☐

2. We went on Saturday ☐

3. We saw monkeys ☐

4. Would you like to be a clown ☐

5. We ate cotton candy ☐

6. Have you ever had a candy apple ☐

7. I like them ☐

Curriculum Area: Language Arts   **Skills:** Ending Punctuation

Read your favorite story. Describe it by filling in the blanks and circles with **words**, **sentences**, or **pictures**.

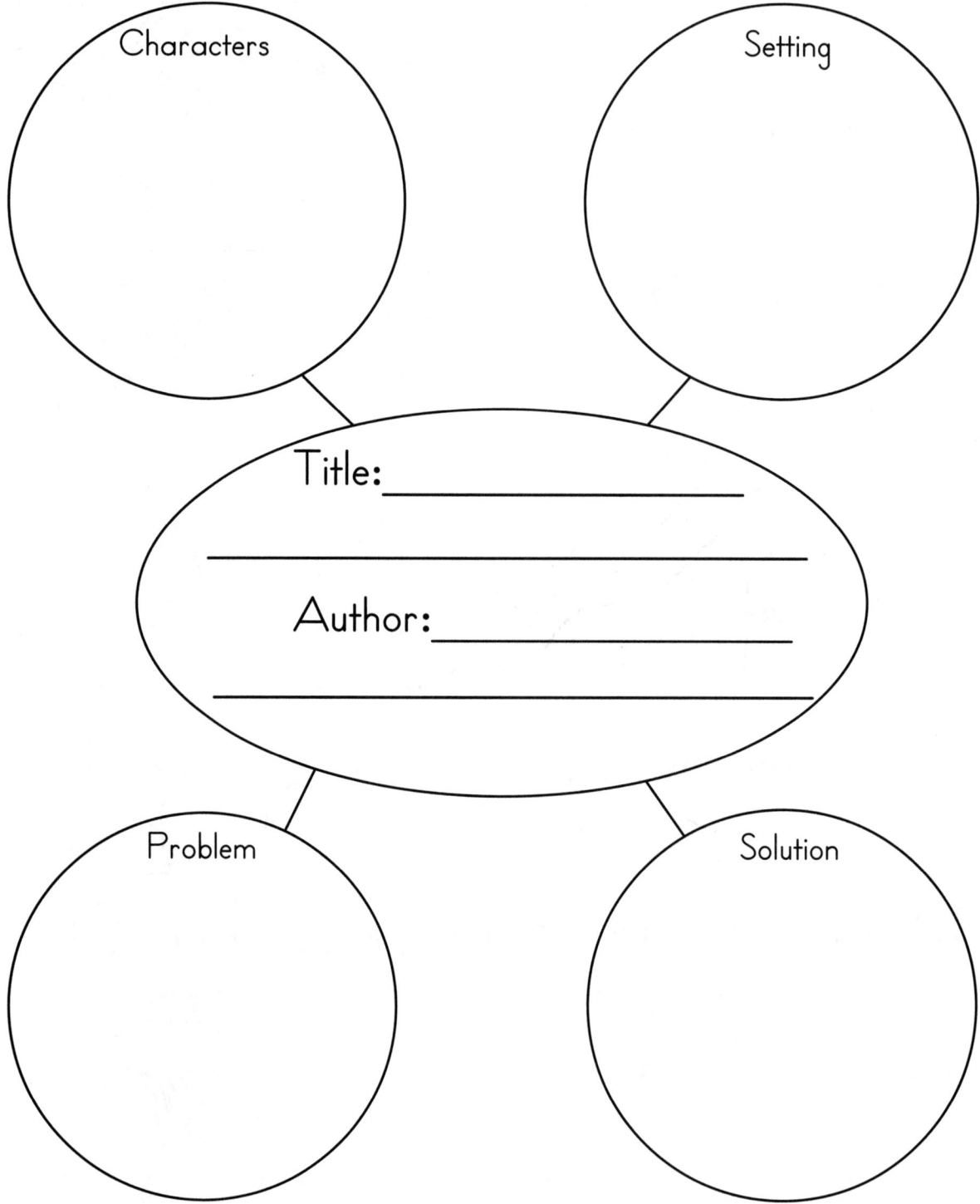

Curriculum Area: Language Arts   **Skills:** Understanding Elements of a Story

Read the stories below. Write the **main idea** of each story in the space provided.

1. Joe had a birthday party. He invited his friends. He got presents. He ate cake and ice cream.

_____
_____
_____
_____
_____

2. Teena wore a costume. She went from house to house. People gave her candy. It was Halloween.

_____
_____
_____
_____
_____

Curriculum Area: Language Arts **Skills:** Reading Comprehension, Recognizing Main Ideas

Read the story. Then answer the questions.

Six bunnies lived in the forest. Two of them were girls. The bunnies went out to see the forest. They got lost. They tried to find their way home. Their mother found them and took them home. They were very happy.

1. How many bunnies lived in the forest?
_____
_____
_____

2. How many bunnies were girls?
_____
_____
_____

3. What happened to the bunnies?
_____
_____

Write a **complete sentence** about each picture.

Curriculum Area: Language Arts   **Skills:** Composing Sentences

Read each story. Write the correct answer on the lines.

1. We went walking. We heard the leaves rustling. We went to see what the noise was. We saw a long bushy gray tail.

   What did we see? _____

   a rabbit   a bird   a squirrel

2. Mrs. Martin reads to us everyday. She holds something in her hands. It has words, pictures, and pages.

   What is she holding? _____

   a pencil   a book   an apple

3. Judy found something soft and furry. She picked it up and rubbed it. It made a purring sound.

   What did Judy find? _____

   a kitten   a dog   a doll

Curriculum Area: Language Arts   **Skills:** Using Context Clues, Reading Comprehension

Pull-Out Answer Key

Page 1
The letters of the alphabet should be printed on the lines in both uppercase and lowercase letters.

Page 2
chick
duck
horse
rabbit

Page 3
1. **f**an   2. **g**ate   3. **m**oon
4. **r**ug   5. **s**eal   6. **b**oat
7. **w**agon 8. **l**eaf   9. **d**eer

Page 4
1. **b**oat   2. **c**ap   3. **m**eat
4. **h**at   5. **b**ook   6. **b**ug
7. **s**un   8. **t**op   9. **c**ake

Page 5
1. bu**s**   2. soa**p**   3. ca**p**
4. lea**f**   5. lio**n**   6. we**b**
7. le**g**   8. dru**m**   9. boo**k**

Page 6
1. c**a**t   2. d**o**ll   3. f**i**sh
4. h**a**t   5. t**o**p   6. d**u**ck
7. sl**e**d   8. t**e**nt   9. cl**o**ck

Page 7

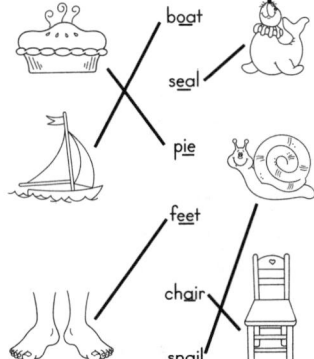

Page 8
A line should be drawn between the following:
  bear — chair
  coat — boat
  cat — hat
  egg — leg
  wig — pig

Page 9

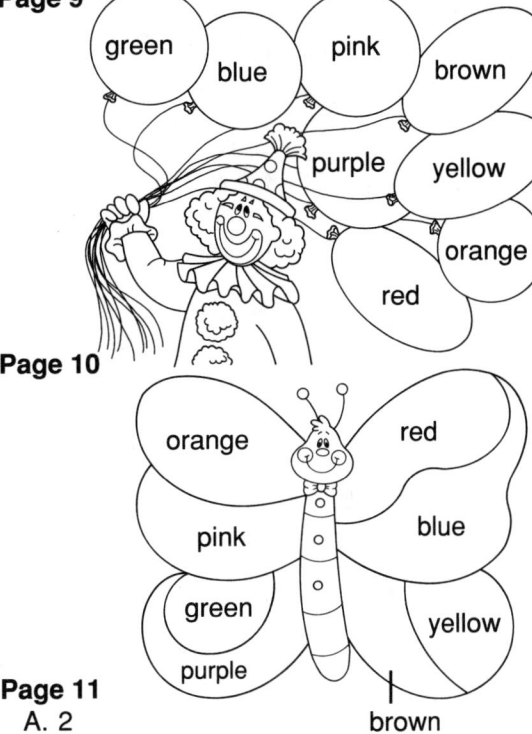

Page 10
(butterfly colored: orange, red, pink, blue, green, yellow, purple, brown)

Page 11
A. 2
   3
   1
B. 1
   3
   2
C. 3
   1
   2
D. 3
   2
   1

Page 12
Draw a circle around the following pictures:
  1. Steve played basketball.
  4. Sue can ride a bike.
  6. Fish can live in the ocean.
Place an X on the following pictures:
  2. Rabbit and Turtle raced.
  3. The bear had a party.
  5. Snail and Worm went to school.

Page 13
A picture should be drawn as instructed.

A

© Carson-Dellosa Publ. CD-6857

Page 14
Answers may be in any order within the categories:

Winter Things
1. mittens
2. snowman
3. sled

Summer Things
1. sunburn
2. pool
3. beach ball

Spring Things
1. flowers
2. Easter
3. showers

Fall Things
1. turkey
2. pumpkins
3. football

Page 15
1. dog + house
2. foot + ball
3. fish + bowl
4. sand + box
5. rain + bow
6. suit + case

Page 16
1. I'm
2. We've
3. couldn't
4. We're
5. we'll

Page 17
1. she laid some eggs.
2. went on a picnic.

Page 18
January
February
March
April
May
June
July
August
September
October
November
December

Page 19
Sunday
Monday
Tuesday
Wednesday
Thursday
Friday
Saturday

Page 20
1. He
2. They
3. She
4. We

Page 21
1. excited
2. sad
3. happy

Page 22
1. **D**id **J**udy name her kitten **F**luffy?
2. **T**oday is **T**uesday.
3. **W**ill it snow in **J**anuary?

Page 23
1. question mark
2. period
3. period
4. question mark
5. period
6. question mark
7. period

Page 24
A title of a book and the author should be written on the lines in the oval. Words, sentences, and pictures should be inside each circle, describing the corresponding heading.

Page 25
1. Jack had a birthday party.
2. It was Halloween.

Page 26
1. Six.
2. Two.
3. They got lost.

Page 27
A complete sentence should be written about each picture. Answers will vary.

Page 28
1. a squirrel
2. a book
3. a kitten

Page 29

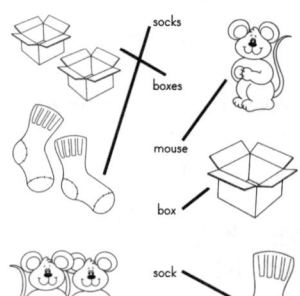

Page 30

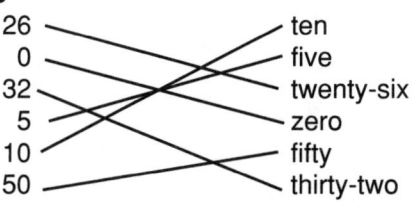

Page 31
The next pattern part for each row should be:
1. rectangle
2. square
3. oval
4. heart
5. figure eight

Page 32
The missing pattern part for each row should be:
1. circle
2. triangle
3. rectangle
4. heart
5. star

Page 33
Numbers should be filled in to complete the sequence from 1 to 100.

Page 34
A. 1, 3, 5, **7**, 9, **11**, **13**, 15
B. 3, 6, 9, **12**, **15**, 18, 21, **24**, 27
C. 2, 4, 6, **8**, **10**, **12**, 14, 16
D. 55, 50, **45**, 40, 35, **30**, **25**, 20
E. 100, 200, **300**, 400, **500**, 600, **700**
F. 67, 68, **69**, **70**, **71**, 72, **73**

Page 35
A. 5, 10, **15**, **20**, **25**, 30, **35**, **40**, 45, 50, 55, **60**, **65**, 70, 75, **80**, 85, 90, **95**, 100
B. 10, **20**, **30**, **40**, 50, **60**, **70**, 80, **90**, 100
C. 2, 4, 6, **8**, 10, **12**, **14**, 16, **18**, 20, 22, **24**, **26**, **28**, 30
D. 3, 6, **9**, **12**, 15, 18, **21**, 24, **27**, 30

Page 36
26 — ten
0 — five
32 — twenty-six
5 — zero
10 — fifty
50 — thirty-two

Page 37
A. 26, **30**   **41**, 29   **50**, 20   99, **100**
B. 11, **19**   **67**, 57   **84**, 48   **72**, 27
C. **43**, 34   10, **60**   50, **75**   **38**, 28
D. **0**, 10   70, **50**   **15**, 30   50, **25**
E. 48, **24**   **16**, 32   **36**, 72   **40**, 80
F. **29**, 58   **19**, 38   42, **21**   100, **50**

Page 38
The dots should be connected from 5 to 100 to form an octopus.

Page 39

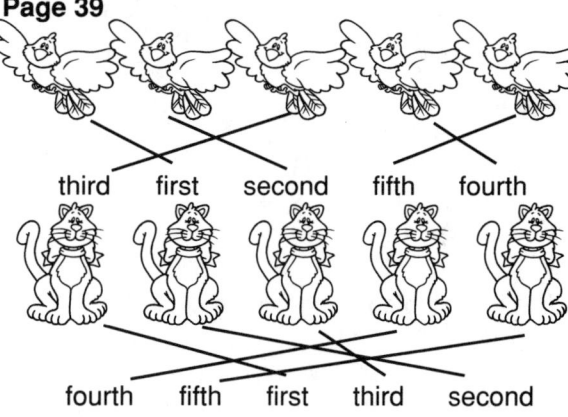

Page 40
1. Thursday
2. 4
3. 4
4. Thursdays

Page 41
A. 5:00   B. 3:00
C. 6:00   D. 7:30
E. 10:30   F. 12:00

Page 42
Hands should be drawn on each of the clocks to indicate the correct time.

Page 43

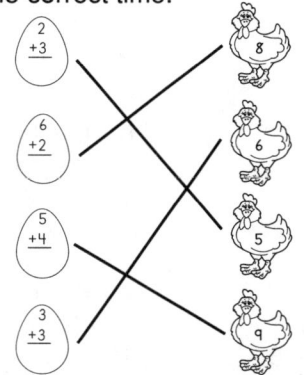

© Carson-Dellosa Publ. CD-6857

Page 44
The answers along the path are as follows:
9, 9, 4, 7, 8

Page 45

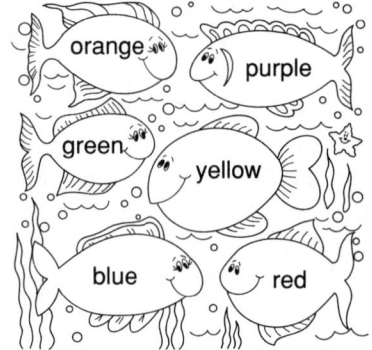

Page 46
A. 6   B. 7   C. 3   D. 8
E. 4   F. 2   G. 1   H. 8
I. 5   J. 10   K. 4   L. 0
M. 7   N. 4   O. 9   P. 7

Page 47
The following coins should be circled:
A. 1 dime, 1 nickel
B. 1 quarter, 1 penny
C. 1 quarter, 1 dime, 1 nickel, 2 pennies
D. 2 quarters, 1 nickel, 1 penny
E. 1 quarter, 1 dime, 3 pennies

Page 48
Answers will vary, but the top graph should be filled with 7 tally marks and the bottom graph should have the corresponding squares filled.

Page 49
A. 63   B. 50
C. 12   D. 39
E. 44   F. 98

Page 50
A. 86   B. 18
C. 72   D. 30
E. 93   F. 24

Page 51
A. $7 + 5 = 12$ B. $8 + 6 = 14$
   $5 + 7 = 12$ $6 + 8 = 14$
   $12 - 7 = 5$ $14 - 6 = 8$
   $12 - 5 = 7$ $14 - 8 = 6$
C. $6 + 5 = 11$ D. $9 + 4 = 13$
   $5 + 6 = 11$ $9 + 4 = 13$
   $11 - 5 = 6$ $13 - 9 = 4$
   $11 - 6 = 5$ $13 - 4 = 9$

Page 52
A. 13   B. 14   C. 11   D. 13
E. 15   F. 14   G. 16   H. 15
I. 11   J. 12   K. 13   L. 17

Page 53
A. $\frac{1}{2}$ B. $\frac{1}{4}$
C. $\frac{3}{4}$ D. $\frac{1}{3}$
E. $\frac{2}{4}$ F. $\frac{2}{4}$

Page 54
A. $5 + 5 = 10$ B. $3 + 6 = 9$
C. $6 + 5 = 11$ D. $7 + 7 = 14$
E. $2 + 7 = 9$ F. $0 + 4 = 4$
G. $3 + 9 = 12$ H. $7 + 3 = 10$
I. $9 + 8 = 17$ J. $8 + 7 = 15$
K. $8 + 6 = 14$ L. $9 + 3 = 12$

Page 55
A. 8   B. 6   C. 8
D. 7   E. 4   F. 8
G. 2   H. 0   I. 5

Page 56
A. 90   B. 83   C. 78
D. 97   E. 34   F. 54
G. 99   H. 89   I. 66

Page 57
A. 39   B. 60   C. 20
D. 30   E. 19   F. 44
G. 52   H. 10   I. 51

Page 58
A. 4
B. 8
C. 5
D. 11

Page 59
A. 20¢
B. Yes
C. 35¢
   15¢

Page 60
A. 14, Steve, John
B. 18, 12, 14, 30

Continue the pattern. Draw the **next** pattern part in the box.

A.

B.

C.

D.

E.

Curriculum Area: Math **Skills:** Patterning

Draw in the **missing pattern** part for each row.

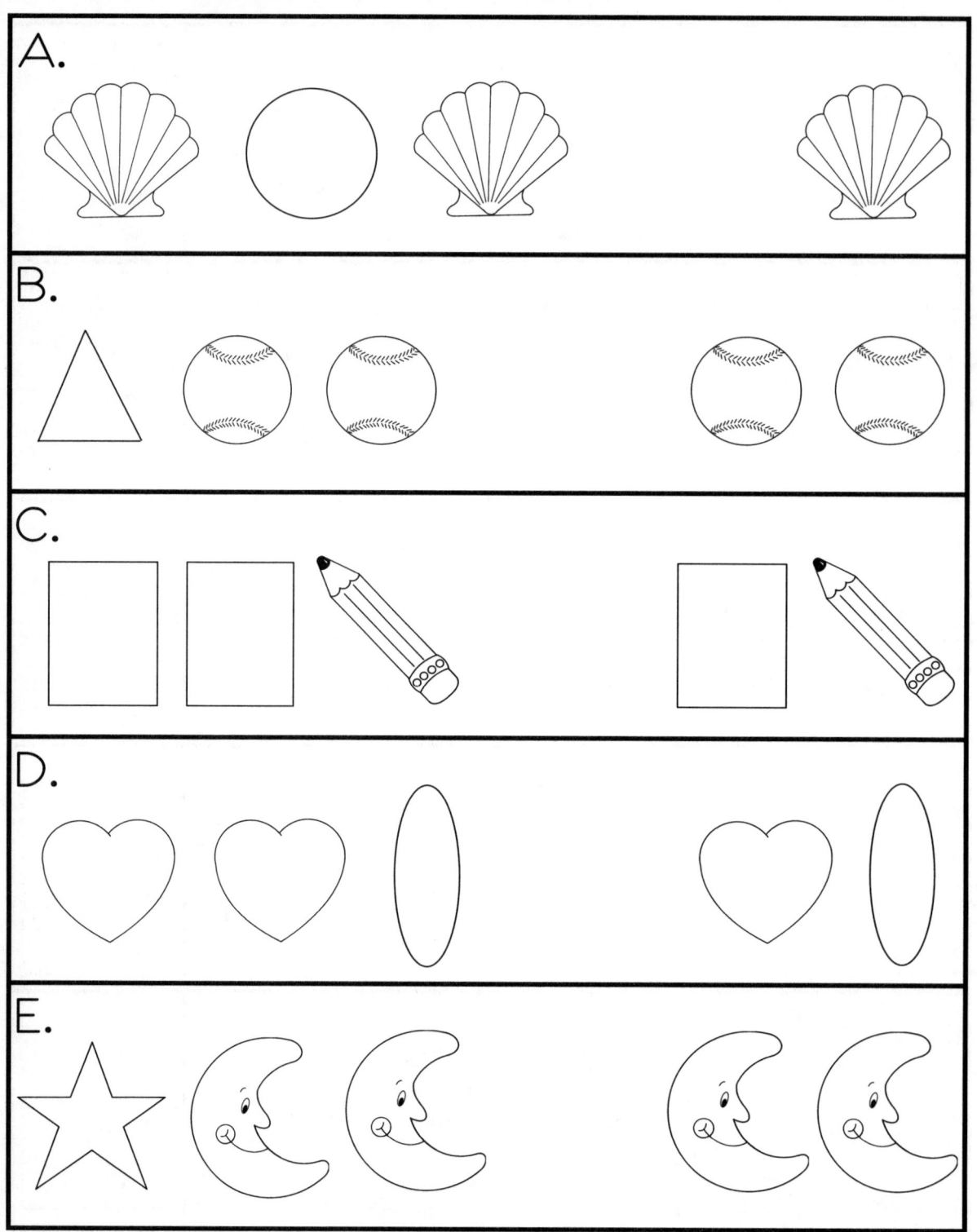

Fill in the missing **numerals to 100**.

1	2	3					8	9	
11		13			16		18		
21	22			25		27			30
	32	33			36		38		40
41	42		44	45		47	48		
51			54		56				60
	62	63		65			68	69	
71			74	75		77		79	80
	82			85	86	87		89	
91			94		96				100

Curriculum Area: Math **Skills:** Sequencing Numerals, Counting

Fill in the missing numerals. Watch for the patterns.

A. 1, 3, 5, _____, 9, _____, _____, 15

B. 3, 6, 9, _____, _____, 18, 21, _____, 27

C. 2, 4, 6, _____, _____, _____, 14, 16

D. 55, 50, _____, 40, 35, _____, _____, 20

E. 100, 200, _____, 400, _____, 600, _____

F. 67, 68, _____, _____, _____, 72, _____

Curriculum Area: Math **Skills:** Sequencing Numerals, Counting

Follow the instructions above each group of numerals.

A. Count by **fives** to 100. Fill in the missing numerals.
5, 10, ____, ____, ____, 30, ____, ____, 45, 50, 55, ____, ____, 70, 75, ____, 85, 90, ____, 100

B. Count by **tens** to 100. Fill in the missing numerals.
10, ____, ____, ____, 50, ____, ____, 80, ____, 100

C. Count by **twos** to 30. Fill in the missing numerals.
2, 4, 6, ____, 10, ____, ____, 16, ____, 20, 22, ____, ____, ____, 30

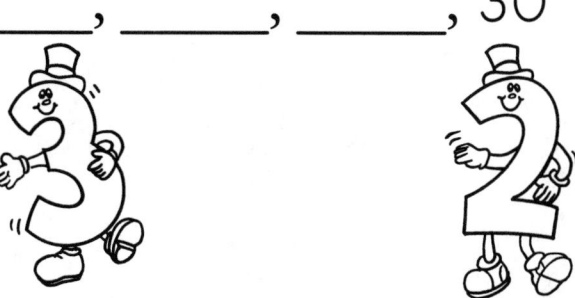

D. Count by **threes** to 30. Fill in the missing numerals.
3, 6, ____, ____, 15, 18, ____, 24, ____, 30

Curriculum Area: Math **Skills:** Step Counting, Sequencing Numerals

Draw a line from each numeral to its matching number word.

26   ten

0   five

32   twenty-six

5   zero

10   fifty

50   thirty-two

Curriculum Area: Math   **Skills:** Matching Numerals to Numeral Words

Follow the directions above each pair of numbers.

Circle the number that is **greater** in each box.

A.	26, 30	41, 29	50, 20	99, 100
B.	11, 19	67, 57	84, 48	72, 27
C.	43, 34	10, 60	50, 75	38, 28

Circle the number that is **less** in each box.

D.	0, 10	70, 50	15, 30	50, 25
E.	48, 24	16, 32	36, 72	40, 80
F.	29, 58	19, 38	42, 21	100, 50

Curriculum Area: Math   **Skills:** Identifying Numbers as Greater Than or Less Than

Count by fives. Start at the "★" and connect the dots from 5 to 100 to make an animal from the sea. Color the picture.

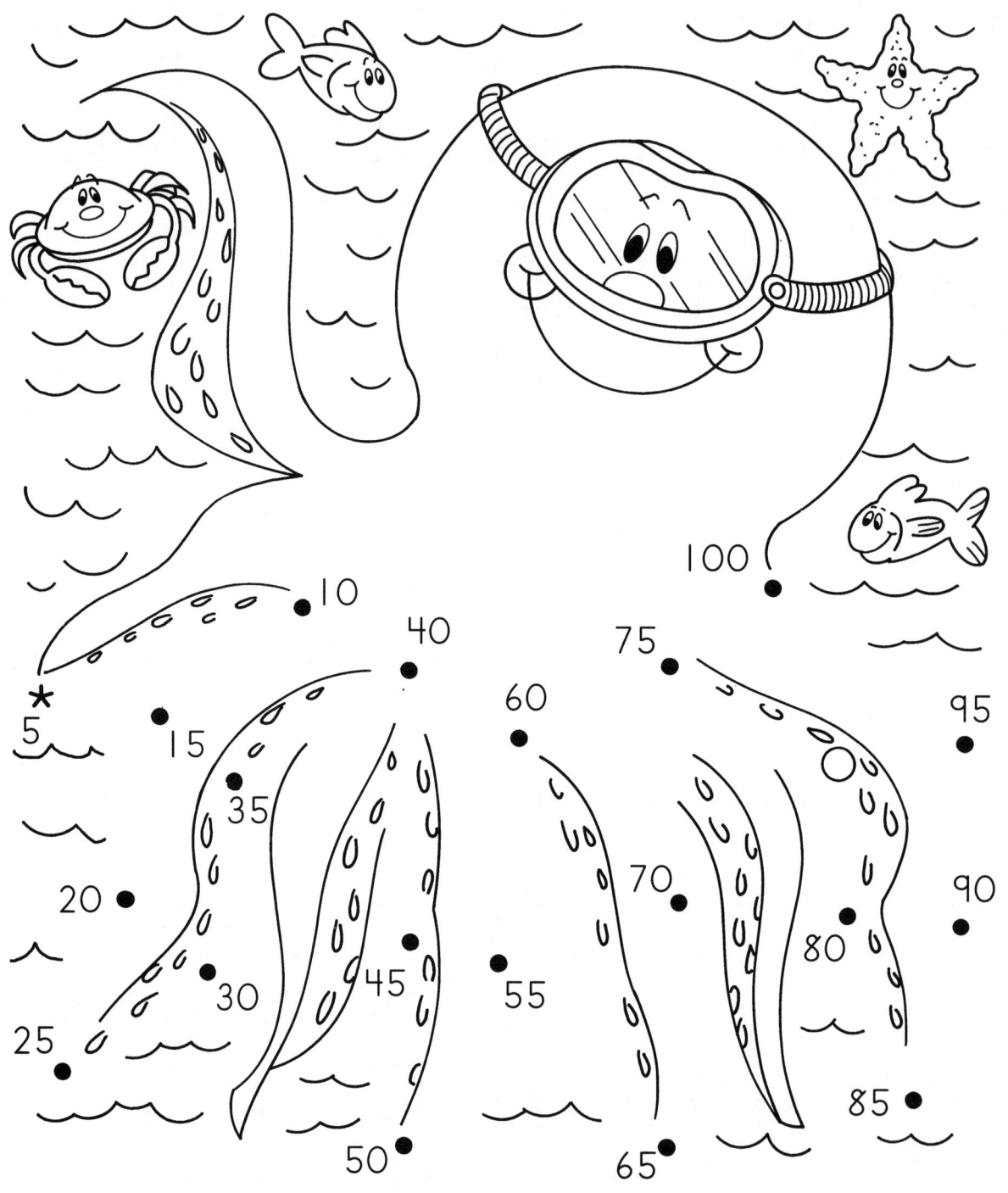

Curriculum Area: Math **Skills:** Ordering Numerals, Counting By Fives

Use the picture below to help you match the animals in each row with the word that shows its place in line.

Trace the numeral 1, then complete the **calendar** by filling in the missing numerals 2-30. Answer the questions below.

\multicolumn{7}{c}{June}
Sun.	Mon.	Tues.	Wed.	Thurs.	Fri.	Sat.
			1			

1. On what day of the week does June end?

2. How many Tuesdays are in June?

3. How many Saturdays are in June?

4. Are there more Thursdays or Sundays?

Curriculum Area: Math   **Skills:** Reading A Calendar, Counting

Trace the answer for the first clock, then write the **time** you see on each clock.

A. 5:00   B. _____

C. _____   D. _____

E. _____   F. _____

Curriculum Area: Math   **Skills:** Telling Time to the Hour and Half Hour

Draw hands on each clock to show the correct time.

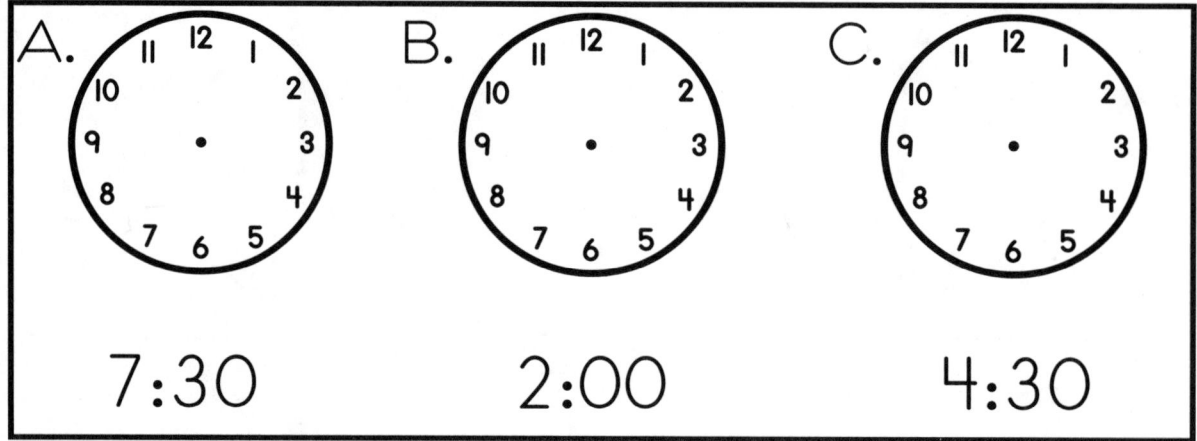
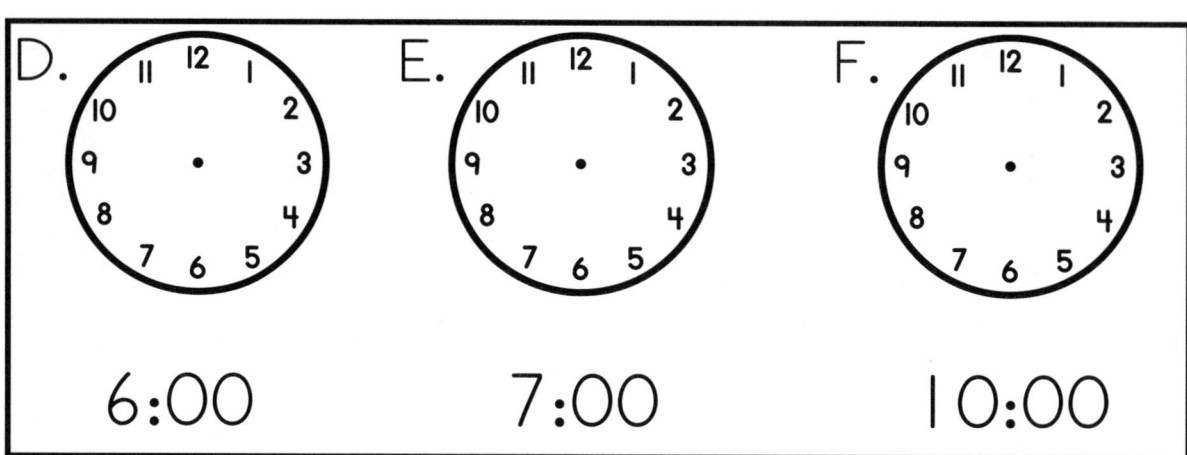
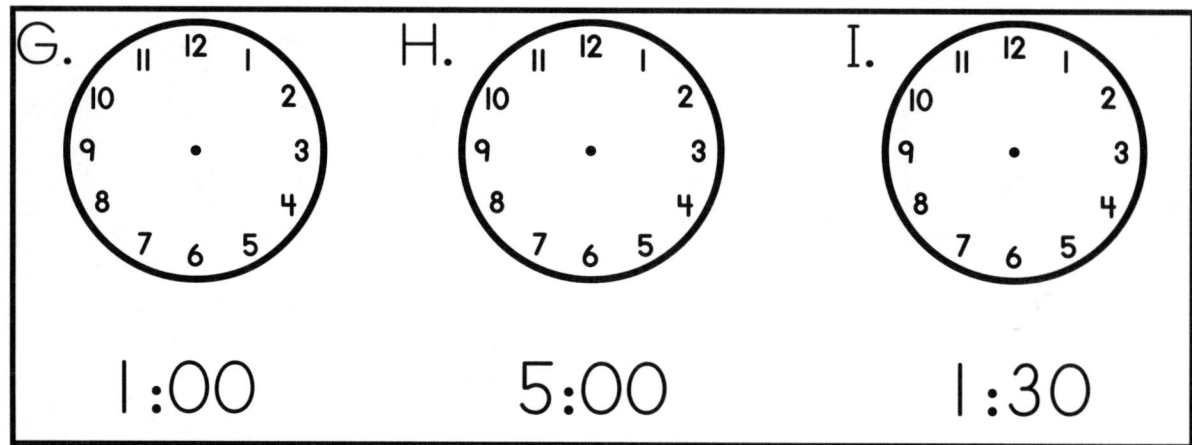

Curriculum Area: Math **Skills:** Telling Time to the Hour and Half Hour

Add or **subtract** to solve the problems and then color the fish using the key below.

Key

10 = yellow	13 = orange
11 = blue	14 = red
12 = purple	15 = green

Curriculum Area: Math **Skills:** Adding and Subtracting With No Regrouping, Coloring

Add or **subtract**. Watch the signs.

A. 4
   +2

    6

B. 0
   +7

    7

C. 1
   +2

    3

D. 9
   -1

   10

E. 8
   -4

   12

F. 9
   -7

G. 7
   -6

H. 0
   +8

    8

I. 8
   -3

J. 4
   +6

K. 9
   -5

L. 0
   -0

    0

M. 8
   -1

    9

N. 10
   -6

O. 8
   +1

    9

P. 3
   +4

    7

Curriculum Area: Math   **Skills:** Adding, Subtracting

Circle the **coins** needed for each piggy bank.

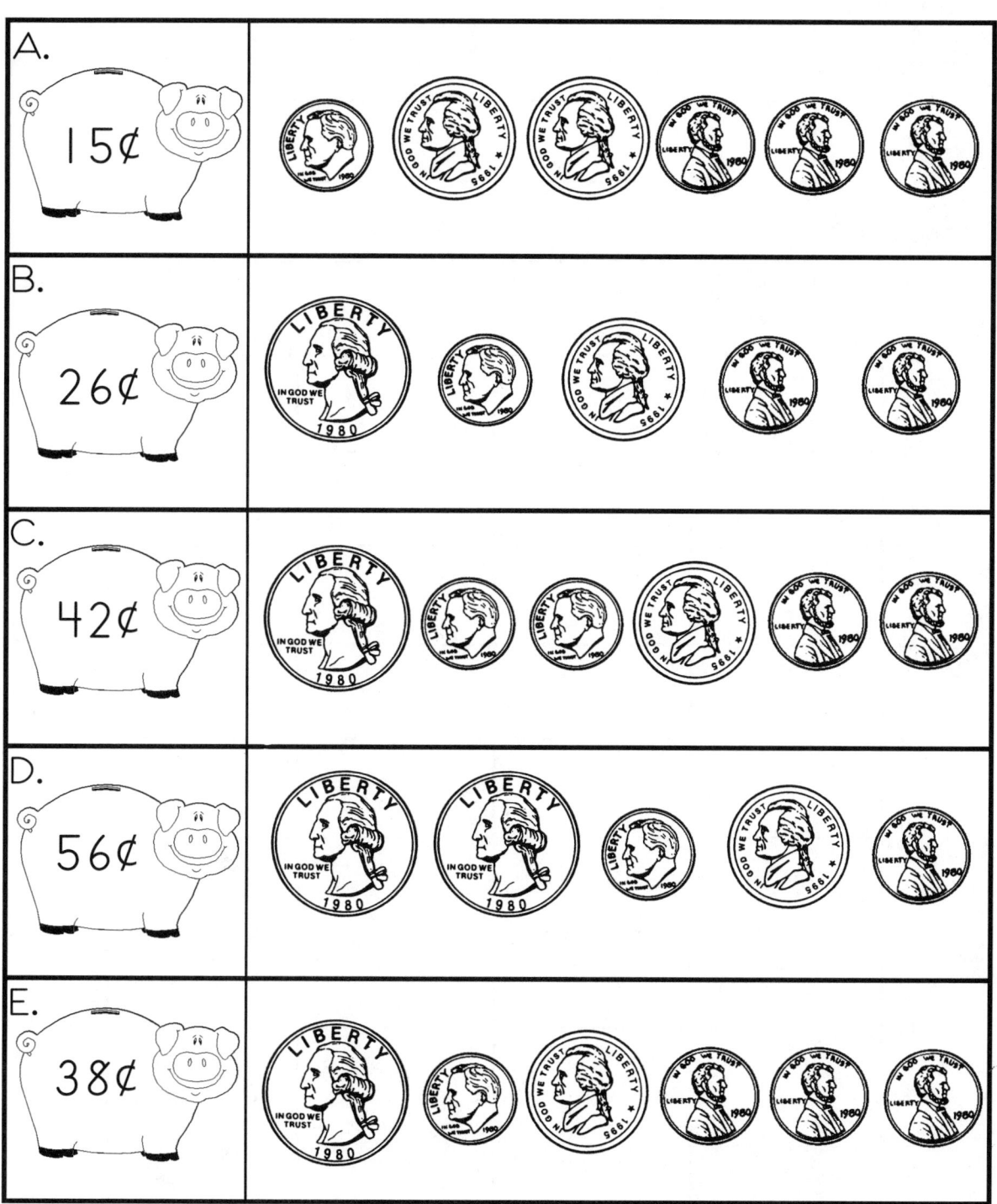

Curriculum Area: Math   **Skills:** Recognizing Coin Values, Counting

Ask seven friends which sport they like best. In the box below, put a tally mark beside the sport each one likes. Then count the tally marks and color in the **graph**.

Baseball		
Basketball		
Football		
Soccer		

Curriculum Area: Math   **Skills:** Creating and Reading Graphs

Write the **numeral** each group shows.

tens	ones
6	3

tens	ones
5	0

A. _____   B. _____

tens	ones
1	2

tens	ones
3	9

C. _____   D. _____

tens	ones
4	4

tens	ones
9	8

E. _____   F. _____

Curriculum Area: Math   **Skills:** Writing Numerals, Understanding Place Value

For each box, write the numeral shown as tens and ones.

A.
tens	ones

86

B.
tens	ones

18

C.
tens	ones

72

D.
tens	ones

30

E.
tens	ones

93

F.
tens	ones

24

Curriculum Area: Math   **Skills:** Writing Numerals, Understanding Place Value

Write the missing numerals in each **number family**.

A. family: 12, 7, 5

7 + ____ = 12

5 + 7 = ____

12 − ____ = 5

12 − 5 = ____

B. family: 14, 8, 6

8 + ____ = 14

6 + 8 = ____

14 − 6 = ____

14 − ____ = 6

C. family: 11, 6, 5

6 + 5 = ____

5 + ____ = 11

11 − 5 = ____

11 − ____ = 5

D. family: 13, 9, 4

9 + ____ = 13

____ + 4 = ____

13 − ____ = 4

13 − ____ = 9

Curriculum Area: Math   **Skills:** Adding, Subtracting, Working With Number Families

Add to solve the problems.

A. 7
    4
   +2
   ___

B. 6
    5
   +3
   ___

C. 4
    4
   +3
   ___

D. 4
    3
   +6
   ___

E. 5
    6
   +4
   ___

F. 7
    5
   +2
   ___

G. 2
    9
   +5
   ___

H. 8
    0
   +7
   ___

I. 4
    2
   +5
   ___

J. 4
    6
   +2
   ___

K. 7
    2
   +4
   ___

L. 8
    8
   +1
   ___

Curriculum Area: Math   **Skills:** Adding Three Digits Equalling More Than Ten

Circle the **fraction** each picture shows.

A.

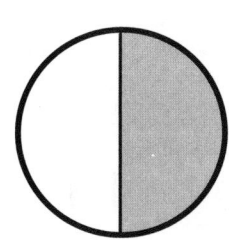

$\frac{1}{3}$ $\frac{1}{4}$ $\frac{1}{2}$

B.

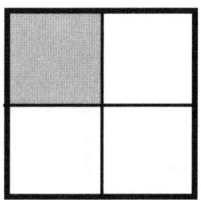

$\frac{1}{3}$ $\frac{1}{4}$ $\frac{2}{4}$

C.

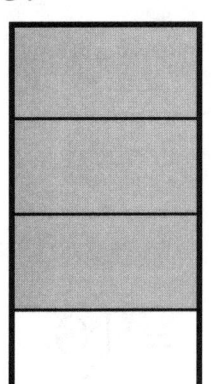

$\frac{2}{3}$ $\frac{3}{4}$ $\frac{2}{4}$

D.

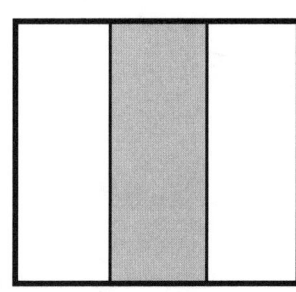

$\frac{1}{3}$ $\frac{1}{4}$ $\frac{2}{4}$

E.

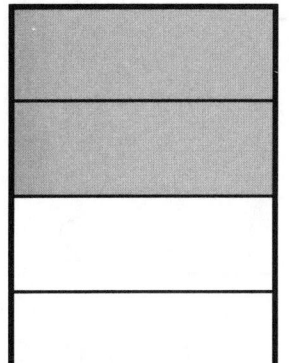

$\frac{2}{3}$ $\frac{3}{4}$ $\frac{2}{4}$

F.

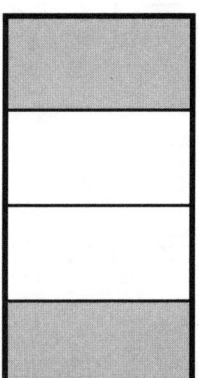

$\frac{1}{3}$ $\frac{1}{4}$ $\frac{2}{4}$

Curriculum Area: Math   **Skills:** Recognizing Fractional Parts of a Whole

Write in the **missing numbers**.

A. $5 + \underline{} = 10$ B. $3 + \underline{} = 9$

C. $6 + \underline{} = 11$ D. $7 + \underline{} = 14$

E. $2 + \underline{} = 9$ F. $0 + \underline{} = 4$

G. $3 + \underline{} = 12$ H. $7 + \underline{} = 10$

I. $9 + \underline{} = 17$ J. $8 + \underline{} = 15$

K. $8 + \underline{} = 14$ L. $9 + \underline{} = 12$

Curriculum Area: Math   **Skills:** Finding Missing Addends

Fill in the **missing numbers**.

A. 16
   -☐
   ───
    8

B. 15
   -☐
   ───
    9

C. 17
   -☐
   ───
    9

D. 14
   -☐
   ───
    7

E. 10
   -☐
   ───
    6

F.   8
   -☐
   ───
    0

G.   6
   -☐
   ───
    4

H.   9
   -☐
   ───
    9

I. 12
   -☐
   ───
    7

Curriculum Area: Math **Skills:** Finding Missing Subtrahends

Add to solve the problems.

A. 40
   +50
   ___

B. 80
   + 3
   ___

C. 47
   +31
   ___

D. 51
   +46
   ___

E. 23
   +11
   ___

F. 42
   +12
   ___

G. 39
   +60
   ___

H. 32
   +57
   ___

I. 33
   +33
   ___

Curriculum Area: Math **Skills:** Adding Two Digits With No Regrouping

Subtract to solve the problems.

A. 69
   -30
   ___

B. 80
   -20
   ___

C. 32
   -12
   ___

D. 40
   -10
   ___

E. 59
   -40
   ___

F. 75
   -31
   ___

G. 92
   -40
   ___

H. 29
   -19
   ___

I. 82
   -31
   ___

Look at each centimeter ruler. Write the length of each object in **centimeters**.

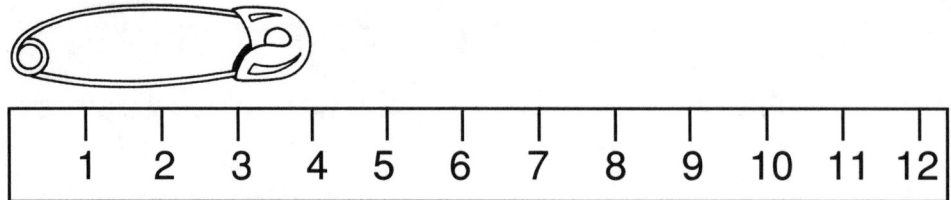

A. _____ cm

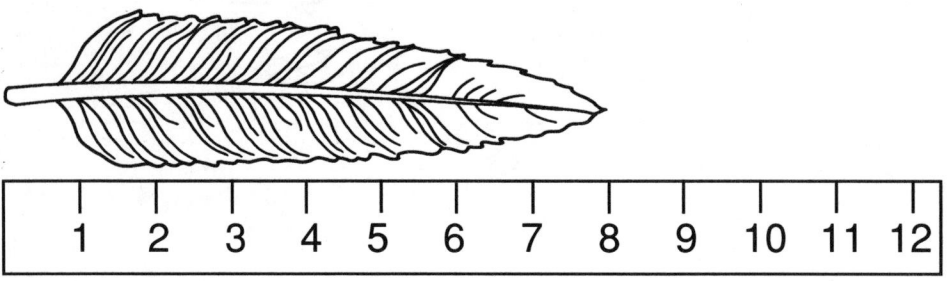

B. _____ cm

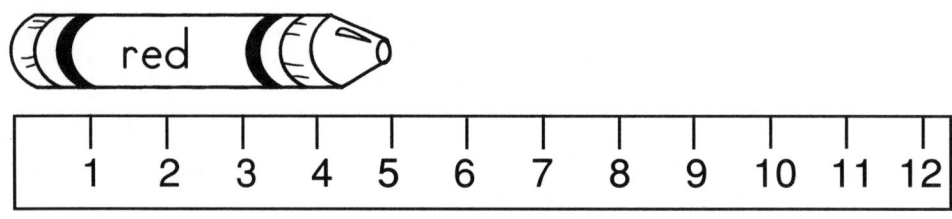

C. _____ cm

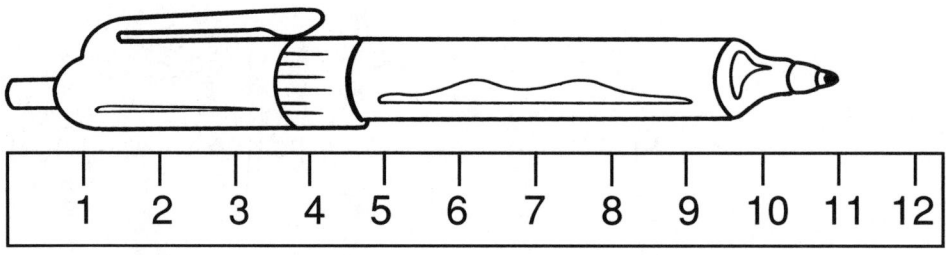

D. _____ cm

Curriculum Area: Math   **Skills:** Measuring in Centimeters

Solve the **word problems**.

A. Susan had a nickel. She found another nickel. Her mother gave her a dime for taking out the trash. How much money does she have now?

_____ ¢

B. Tim wants to buy ice cream at lunch. Lunch costs 50¢ and ice cream costs 25¢. If Tim has $1.00 does he have enough to buy both?

Yes   No

C. Mary took 50¢ to the store. She spent 10¢ for candy, 10¢ for popcorn, and 15¢ for a drink. How much did she spend?

_____ ¢

How much does she have left?

_____ ¢

Curriculum Area: Math   **Skills:** Solving Money Word Problems

Read the stories and solve the **word problems**.

A. Steve had 6 marbles. Mike had 5 marbles. John had 3 marbles.

How many marbles did they have altogether? _____

Who had the most marbles? _____

Who had the least marbles? _____

B. At school, we checked our closet. We found 10 coats with hoods. There were 8 coats without hoods. There were 6 ski caps and 6 umbrellas.

How many coats were there in all? _____

How many umbrellas and ski caps were there altogether? _____

How many coats without hoods and umbrellas were there? _____

How many things were in the closet in all? _____

Curriculum Area: Math   **Skills:** Solving Word Problems